Wording Around with Prose:

Getting a First Draft Out of Your Head and Onto the Page

Kathy Mac

Wording Around Press
2020

Cover image and design by Delaney Crawford, Milly Squires, and Katy Johnson. Cover model Neomi Iancu Haliva.
Final Copy Editing & Proofreading by Dominic Kent, Carly Mason, and Salima Tourkmani-MacDonald.
Hard Copy preparation by Claude Chartier, Neomi Iancu Haliva, and Rae Thomas.
Digital preparation by Sara Lamk, Erika Ruiz Arenas, and Caelin Sullivan.

Wording Around Press
345 Oxford Street
Fredericton, NB, Canada
E3B 2W6

Wording Around with Prose: Getting a First Draft Out of your Head and onto the Page. / Kathy Mac
November 2020.

book: isbn 978-1-7773739-0-0
ebook: isbn 978-1-7773739-1-7

Contents

Land Acknowledgment, Thanks 1
Dedication, In Memoriam 2
Preface 3
1. Why We Write, and Why We Don't 6
2. Time Management Tips and Tantrums 10
3. Research 14
Part A: Overarching Research 14
Part B: Internal Research 16
4. Pre-writing 18
5. Point of View 21
Part A: Narrator 21
Part B: Parataxis and Hypotaxis 24
6. Primary Characters 28
Part A: The Protagonist 28
Part B: The Telling Detail 32
7. Openings 36
8. Plot and Structure 40
Part A: Plot 40
Part B: Structure 41
9. Secondary Characters 48
Part A: Types 48
Part B: Diversity 50
10. Conflict 53
11. Setting 56
12. Dialogue 60
Conclusion: The Story So Far 62

List of Prompts....64
Suggested Resources....65
Appendix 1: Character Questionnaire....67
Appendix 2: Seven Basic Plots....69
Works and Authors Cited, by Chapter....70

Land Acknowledgement

Wording Around with Prose was written in Fredericton, New Brunswick, Canada. Fredericton is in the traditional territory of the Wolastoqiyik, (Maliseet) whose ancestors, along with the Mi'Kmaq and Passamaquoddy Nations signed Peace and Friendship Treaties with the British Crown in the 1700s.

Thanks

Wording Around with Prose wouldn't be in front of you now if it weren't for St. Thomas University Fredericton's ENGL 3153: Literary Publishing class, doughty literary warriors who came back to university in autumn 2020 even though in-person classes had to be cancelled due to COVID-19:

> Claude Chartier, Delaney Crawford, Neomi Iancu Haliva, Katy Johnson, Dominic Kent, Sara Lamk, Carly Mason, Erika Ruiz Arenas, Milly Squires, Caelin Sullivan, Rae Thomas, and Salima Tourkmani-MacDonald.

Thanks to Bridget Canning (author of *The Greatest Hits of Wanda Janes*) for compiling the fifteen questions in the middle part of the Character Questionnaire (appendix 1), including question 15 "Compare this character to a door," which she got from Cassie Stocks (author of *Dance, Gladys, Dance*). There are thousands of such questionnaires online; but this one is the best.

Thanks also go out to editor and teaching assistant Jamie Kitts, who kept us in line online and helped prepare the manuscript in August, created the Wording Around website, and undertook a hundred other tasks to keep the project of publishing this on track.

And thank you to AJ Ripley who came up with the name "Wording Around," lo those many years when they were my creative writing course assistant and we needed a title for a blog. (Congratulations, Dr. AJ!)

Dedication

The book version of *Wording Around with Prose* is dedicated to the participants who made it to the end of the Wording Around with Prose course in Spring 2020. It would have been lonely teaching without you:

Shari Andrews, Zev Bagel, Sandra Bunting, Jim Doyle, Brandi Estey-Burt, Barb Fullerton, Linda Glencross, Lori Henderson-Stickles, Albert Katz, Stella MacLean, Colleen Marie, Michelle McLean, Denise McClure, Rick McConnell, Mad McDaniel, Denise McClure, Lauren Michelle McWilliam, Mary Mesheau, Carlos Morales, Melanie Mosher, Janet Patch, Pat Post, Kim Renton, Brigitte Rivers, Edrick Robichaud, Louise Somerville, Jane Tims, Maria Thibault Nason, Ana Watts, David Watts, and others who tuned in for many of the talks.

In Memoriam

In the pauses from reading *Wording Around with Prose,* please remember Dr. Lissa Beauchamp Desroches, Mary Louise Luck, Sheila Nelles, Joe Blades, or anyone else you knew who died during the COVID-19 lockdown in the spring of 2020.

At the time, memorial services were just not possible, so I ask that you to let the sight of this book remind you to celebrate their lives.

Preface

The Writers' Federation of New Brunswick's 2020 WordSpring Festival "coulda bin a contenda" if it hadn't been cancelled due to the COVID-19 lockdown. Since I was Chair of the Organizing Committee, the cancellation freed up some of my time. I also felt responsible to the members of the WFNB missing out on the festival. That's why I volunteered to provide an online course, and Wording Around with Prose was born.

The course was a better idea than I realized. In late March, we were just starting to realize how long we might be stuck in "social isolation." (That's what we called it then. It took another month or so to be spun into the more user-friendly "physical distancing.") Once Wording Around with Prose ended, I requested evaluations from the participants. In them, I read things like:

> "Your course helped me make it through these strange times; gave some structure to my week; and always left me with something I did not know before." —Jane Tims

> "The content was helpful, your delivery fun, clear, and accessible, and I truly appreciate you offering your time in this way during this stressful and difficult chapter of our lives. Thank you." —Michelle McLean

> "It made me feel close to my friends as I saw them check-in." —Ana Watts

> "Obviously Kathy was thinking of the well-being of people in creating and delivering the course. That was a very generous gift to the world." —Barb Fullerton

I'll let you in on a secret: prepping the classes put structure and meaning back into my weeks too.

The course, which ran from April 6 to May 21, 2020, was presented on Facebook Live. It didn't matter if people couldn't make it for the live feed because Facebook posts recordings pretty much immediately after they're done. A couple of evaluations mentioned how useful it was to be able to rewatch the "lectorials" (less formal than a lecture, less interactive than a tutorial). Anyone could and did access the videos. The largest number of participants was 47 for one lectorial; between 25 and 30 people stuck it out for the whole course.

The text of this book is based on each week's pair of lectorials; I tried to keep them to about twenty minutes each, so the chapters are short. *Wording Around with Prose* includes the first four weeks' worth of notes. (The final three weeks of the course were about editing, a topic for another book on another day.) These chapters provide pointers and pep talks, goals and goads, prompts and resources designed to help you get to the end of a (hairy, baggy, rough) first draft of a long prose project, whether it's a novel, a novella, a collection of stories, a memoir, a travelogue, or some other type of prose fiction or creative nonfiction.

The structure of *Wording Around with Prose* mirrors the writing process. Chapters one through four work through some issues you need to consider on your way to starting a first draft. Chapters five through twelve examine things you need to keep in mind while writing that first draft. The talks on character divided naturally into five topics across three chapters, so I interleaved them between chapters that deal with other elements of writing. I could have written character as one humongous chapter, but the truth is that as we write, we work concurrently on character, and structure, and conflict, and setting, and….

Each chapter begins with a discussion of the topic and then gives a prompt and a resource. If the discussion provided here whets your appetite for the topic, you can follow up by having a look at the resource. Or take your curiosity to the search engine of your choice

A few observations and caveats….

- When a character's gender is non-specific, I refer to them as "they" or "them."
- The "rules" for excellent writing included here should more accurately be called "best practices;" they are mostly always true, but there are exceptions to each of them.
- I use the terms "your project" and "your story" interchangeably; I like "story" better, because even if you're writing creative nonfiction, you're crafting a story, but it's important that both fiction and creative nonfiction authors feel represented.
- Similarly, the word "book" can refer to any digital, audio, or online resource, as well as good old hard copy.
- You'll see "protagonist" more often than "hero" or "heroine," because it is neither genre nor gender specific. When I quote or paraphrase someone else, however, you might see one of the "h' words.

The prompts are designed to help you get on with your first draft. Maybe you'll do them all. Maybe you won't, but you will forge ahead with your project. Or maybe you'll just read this for the quirky prose style. Maybe you'll use the hard copy to shore up your kitchen table's one short leg. Whether your project's no more than neurons firing in your brainpan, or almost all outside your skull already, *Wording Around with Prose* is here to help.

1. Why We Write, and Why We Don't

How do you become a better writer?
Read good books, read books about how to write by good authors, listen to the pros, and write. The main thing you can do to become a better writer is to write.

Just write.

Why Aren't You Writing?
I've heard a lot of reasons why people don't get that story out of their head and onto the page. Here are three of the most common:

1. The project is too big. It's intimidating.
Solution: break it down.

"How do you eat an elephant? One bite at a time."

"Petit a petit l'oiseau fait son nid." (Little by little the bird makes its nest.)

"The journey of a thousand miles begins with a single step."
You don't need to sit down intending to write a novel or even a chapter. You can sit down to write a sentence. Maybe the next one. The one after that. Enough of those, and you'll have finished a page, and then a chapter, and eventually, your whole project will be done.

2. You feel you're not a good enough storyteller or writer.
You know the passive voice is overused by you, or you ain't sure what's good grammar, or your plot is so thrilling in your head that the story sweeps you away but you get it all down and it's dead on the page, or, or, or….

There are a million aspects of writing we're sure we don't do well, but you'll learn in the doing to tell stories in the active voice, to write correct sentences. You'll carry your readers through a story so exciting they'll never notice the problems you can't help but see yourself.

All of this will come if you put the work in.

3. Turns out, writing is a lot like work.
Yes, it is. And I've got worse news: it doesn't get easier. The better you get at writing, the more sophisticated and subtle your problems become.

Writing is work, but it's engaging work. It's exciting work. Because it's imaginative work. So, don't let the effort required stop you.

Why DO You Write?
This is a far more interesting question. And again, there's a lot of possible answers. Here are two of the most common:

- You have something to say (though you may not know what that is when you start, or even halfway through).
- You are a storyteller.

Why Read This Book?
If the best way to become a better writer is to write, then why bother with this, or any other, book about writing?

Wording Around with Prose will introduce you, in a methodical way, to ideas about the craft of writing that will short-cut some of the learning curve. Things that you might discover on your own in a couple of years, you can find out now. Some of these skills will be important to you immediately. Others won't, yet… but someday, they probably will. However, which ones are important to you now and which are little literary time capsules will vary from person to person.

In any case, take advantage of the knowledge in this book. It will accelerate your development as a writer.

Prompt: Free Write for 30 Minutes

Set a timer and write for at least 30 minutes. Write down everything that comes to mind with no particular goal, and don't stop writing. If you get stuck, just repeat the word you just wrote until you think of something else. If you're on a roll when the timer goes off at the end, keep going. The point of this exercise is to turn off your internal editors and critics and let your imagination be the driver.

This might be the most difficult prompt in the book. But it is also very rewarding. People find it hard to give up conscious control and just let ideas flow. Our busy brains tend to break into the process and tell us "This is dumb. My writing is bad. I'm not doing it right. This is a waste of time." Ignore the busy brain. Just write, and let those obstructive thoughts sift down and away, like sediment falling through the ocean. After a while, you'll find yourself in literary *terra incognito*, and you'll start being surprised by the images that arise. One student, Janet Patch, observed that while working on the setting for her story during this exercise, her characters gave her a tour.

You can free write at any point in your project – to get you started, if you are stuck, if you need a break from structuring the plot, if your characters won't behave the way you need them to, whenever. You can also do it for any length of time – from a ten-minute warm up to an hour-long exercise. The time it takes to let go of the conscious editor differs from person to person and session to session.

Resource

"NaNo Prep 101 Workshop." *NaNoWriMo,* preview.nanowrimo.org/nano-prep-101.

This is a free downloadable resource posted by the organizers of NaNoWriMo (National Novel Writing Month). NaNo Prep 101 is a self-directed, six-week course chock full of good ideas to prepare you for writing a long piece of prose.

While you're on the NaNoWriMo page, take some time to check out the site. It includes all kinds of taped pep talks from all sorts of writers. Have a look – maybe your favourite living writer has a talk there. National Novel Writing Month is November, Camp NaNo months occur in April and July. They support you in your personal writing challenge. Right now you'll write for thirty minutes. Later, you might write for forty. Later still, you might not stop until you hit 1000 words. Eventually, you could go all the way in the NaNo challenge: 50,000 words in thirty days. A daunting task, but I think you can do it. Eventually.

For now, thirty minutes, no breaks.

2. Time Management Tips and Tantrums

In my experience, it's likely that even your best beloveds won't understand that you're working when you're sitting on the sofa staring into space. They will poke their heads into your room, ask "Where are the twist-ties?" A minimal interruption. Less than fifteen seconds. No harm, right?

Wrong. That break can be like the penny on the railroad track, only the derailed train is a train of thought. No one else can see it, so no one else will respect it, unless you, the author, do. Guard your creative time and teach the people in your household to do the same.

The Cultural Undervaluation of Creative Work

Don't get me started on how people in the business world sees artists. To them, we're "content providers." For example, as of August 2020, Amazon adds about 2,200 books to Kindle every month (Stark Reflections podcast, #149). That's a big part of the reason that creatives – people who do creative work – are consistently underpaid. The quality of the writing suffers because the focus is on producing quantity.

My advice? Don't bend to the pressure to provide content at the expense of making art. Places like Kindle, Kobo, iBooks, and Google Books have empty vessels; authors have the wherewithal to fill them. We don't have to let corporations dictate the speed at which we do so. Resist falling prey to the attitude that your writing is a commodity like a package of screws.

Avoid Comparisonitis

Inside yourself, you will constantly negotiate the tension between quick writing and careful writing. There's a thing called "pulp speed" (a million words a year – the speed at which a pulp fiction writer like Zane Grey wrote). That's one way of approaching your writing career. On the other hand, Eden Robinson spent eight years writing *Son of a Trickster,* currently in production for a CBC TV adaptation. It's a brilliant book. You need to find out for yourself where you're most comfortable on the Pulp–Trickster pace continuum.

What you don't need to do is compare your process, your writing speed, with that of anyone else. Some people will be slower than you. Others faster. Some will get more sales and downloads, others less. Some will make more money, others less. The only measure that matters is your own.

Organize Yourself

Find strategies that allow you to be a writer that work alongside your life commitments.

Here's mine. Because I have this day job which I absolutely adore (as a full-time creative writing prof, I truly won the career lottery in this lifetime), I have less time than I'd like to be a writer. I used to beat myself up about not writing enough. No matter what I was working on, I felt like I should be doing something else. If I was working on a first draft, I'd think I should be finishing something else. If I was sending out submissions, I'd feel like I should be researching a new project.

Eventually, I hit upon a solution. There are, broadly speaking, four parts of a writing project: Research, First Draft, Editing, and Submissions (Publishing). Every month, I focus on one of these: January: Research. February: First Draft. March: Editing. April: Submissions. Then start the cycle again and go through it twice more by the end of the year.

I'm not rabid about it. I don't miss good opportunities for publication if it's not a submission month (April, August, or December), or miss talking to an expert if its not a research month (January, May, September)… But I don't get panicky the way I used to, always thinking I should be doing something else. Every task has its time, and its time will come.

That works for me. Others think I'm nuts, but it makes me feel secure.

Find a solution that works for you. And keep in mind that your writing habits will evolve as your life's circumstances change.

Here's a home truth about me: I struggle with finding time to be creative. Some days I manage it. Other times, I do not. Life is like that. Just make sure you're being kind to yourself and the people you love, while respecting your drive to do creative work.

Prompt: Find a Way to Fit Writing into Your Life

If you haven't already done so, spend some time figuring out when you can fit writing into your life, and then put that schedule into practice.

This might be the most difficult prompt in the book. But it may also be the most important. You may have to revise your expectations a few times until you find habits that work for you. Maybe you can get up fifteen minutes earlier every workday and get some private writing time in then. Maybe it will be Sunday mornings. Maybe you can spend half an hour at your lunch break, three times a week. Maybe you can do three hours a day all week. If so, lucky you!

Try to work towards writing for three hours a day. Or, if you're not able to actually write, read for the project you are writing. Or go for a walk with one of your characters. If you're serious about being a writer, the goal is to spend at least three hours every day being a writer.

Find your times, and then (and this is easy to say but difficult to achieve) work to ensure your family and friends respect it.

Resource

Nancy Pagh. *Write Moves: A Creative Writing Guide and Anthology*. Broadview Press, 2016.

Pagh's book is pretty much the diametric opposite of "NaNo Prep 101." It is assigned in many university creative writing programs, in part because it's not just a very good textbook for developing creative writing skills – that's only the first half. The second half is an anthology of texts that do the things Pagh discusses in the manual half.

3. Research

The most important message about researching your creative writing can be summed up in two words: do it.

That doesn't mean you have to do it all before you settle down to write; you'll probably do some of it then. Maybe not. Maybe you'll do it on days when you're suffering from writer's block. Often you can dissolve writer's block and get started writing again simply by doing some research and finding out a specific fact that bridges reality and fiction.

Part A: Overarching Research

(Research about things EXTERNAL TO your story.)
If you are writing in a genre, you need to understand the masterworks of that genre. You're writing about a child wizard entering a school for magic? Read *The Magicians*, as well as the Harry Potter novels, and if you really want to get brownie points, *Tom Brown's School Days* (Thomas Hughes 1857), and a lot of other books in the genre besides (Tamora Pierce's *Song of the Lioness*, and *Protector of the Small* quartets for example). And no, it's not enough to have watched the movie, if there is a movie.

In the previous chapter, I suggested that you try to block off three hours a day to work on your writing, but that didn't necessarily mean spending three hours sitting at your desk and writing. Reading books relevant to your project is a big part of your writing life.

What's helpful is to join an organization like the Writers' Federation of New Brunswick or the Writers Union of Canada and attend their conferences and webinars to take workshops with a published author working in your genre. Attend literary festivals and sign up for the workshops they offer. Take copious notes. You'll use some of them for years. As you can tell by the List of Works and Authors Cited at the end of this book, a lot of the knowledge I'm presenting here is gleaned from my decades of attending workshops.

If you aren't familiar with a lot of works in your genre, you might not realize that your original idea isn't all that original. Don't get me started on people who prefer to remain ignorant rather than read in their genre. They'll never get to originality because true originality is based on a deep and abiding knowledge of what you're doing. There's no cutting corners here.

For example, I sat in on a workshop recently with an author who wrote a story about someone moving into an old house. The protagonist found a mask in the attic and put it on. In that moment, they took on the (murderous) character of the maker of the mask. Now, this author had never seen Jim Carrey's 1993 movie *The Mask*, let alone read the comics it was based on. Participants in her workshop advised her to do so. A few weeks later she brought a revised version of her story back to the workshop, but it was clear she hadn't looked up the movie, so she still didn't know how derivative her story was.

Of course, there's "nothing new under the sun" (especially not that cliché). I know that it's distressing to find out that your brilliant idea is so good it's been done a hundred times before. The way to solve that problem is to read widely, in your genre, and out of it.

And take heart. It's possible, and even essential, to achieve originality by building on convention. Writing a long project is like baking a loaf of bread. The bakers amongst us know that bread is made up of three ingredients: water, flour, and yeast. If you're lucky, you've also got some oil and some salt. And from those minimal ingredients, a million million different kinds of bread have sprung: everything from bleached white to pumpernickel, from baguette to naan. Writing is like that. There may be a limited number of plots, but there's an infinite number of ways of expressing those plots.

Part B: Internal Research

(Research about things IN your story.)

Don't be satisfied with what "everybody knows" about whatever it is going on in your story. That's called stereotyping, and it makes for boring writing. Also, nothing is more irritating than being represented in a story by a stereotype. (For example: the idea that artists are airheads is a stereotype. Any artist I know who is making a living at their art is pretty canny. They have to be, to be able to continue making art.) Chapter 9 gets into the evils of stereotyping and how to avoid them. For now, I just want to say that, if your characters are going to travel by horse for a couple of weeks, you need to have done that too, or to have talked to someone who is good at it, or to have read, and read widely about it, or done all three. It's amazing how much work is involved in travel by horseback.

Fictions (film especially) are not reliable sources for your research – they've already been shaped into art, so the images there have a metaphorical function that may have nothing to do with reality, like the violence in a Tarantino movie. It's fantasy folks.

Most of your new knowledge won't make it into the final draft of your manuscript. But you need to have it, to be able to pick and choose those necessary bits to go into your book.

For example, Wording Around with Prose student Edrick Robichaud observed: "I've been doing a tremendous amount of research on sailing in the 18th and 19th centuries, and in Wilbur Smith's *Birds of Prey*, he described a frigate sailing through quite a significant storm with her topgallants open and no consideration of how the 30 to 40 foot or so waves were hitting the hull. In retrospect, I think the hero captain here was incompetent and just lucky they weren't either dismasted or broken up." Now that's someone serious about research!

Conclusion

Either form of research – overarching or internal – may come in the form of reading material, experience, interviews, all sorts of sources.

If you do your research on the internet, be careful to understand the reliability of your sources. Remember: all narrators are unreliable to some extent. Even (especially) online experts have agendas to promote.

Prompt: Research Your Genre

You might find this the most difficult prompt in this book because it involves making a substantial time investment. But it amply rewards that investment. Look online for popular works in the genre that you're writing and read several of them. Find a book (or a bunch of books) on writing your genre and read what they consider the essential elements of that genre. Not all resources are created equal, so make sure to check out the authors of these sources to see what they are basing their authority on.

Resource

The resource recommendation for this is to find (a) genre-appropriate book(s) for your project. For some examples, if you are writing: Romance, you'll want to look at Gwen Hayes' *Romancing the Beat*; Horror, you'll want to have Stephen King's *On Writing* (which is also a good all-round writing guide); Fantasy, you'll want to read Diana Wynne Jones' *Tough Guide to Fantasyland*; Quest Adventure, you'll want to get Stephen Vogler's *The Writer's Journey*; etc.

4. Pre-writing

Why Bother with Pre-Writing?

You pre-write to know the world you're building. You pre-write to give your world verisimilitude, to make it real in your mind and your readers' minds. Even if you're basing your writing project on the people and places in the actual, material world, you're choosing from an infinite number of possibilities the telling details that go down on the page. However, as with your research, the unfortunate truth is that you won't know which bit of that mass of preparatory writing provides the telling detail until you've done a bunch that *isn't* as telling or important.

Honestly, the hardest part of any writing is knowing what's precisely enough. If you've left too much on the page, your readers will feel like their intelligence is being insulted and they'll also be bored. If you've provided too little, they'll be mystified.

When you're not sure whether or not a detail belongs, then put it in the first draft; that's what they're for. First drafts are baggy and big and hairy and tentacular. You can always take the extra stuff out in a later draft.

What Happens in Your Head Should Mostly Stay in Your Head

In February 2020, I spent a month at the Dorland Mountain Arts Colony in California. While there, I met the wonderful, venerable, successful author and journalist Edith Hornik Beer. I helped her out with a writing workshop she was hosting, and so I heard a wonderful bit of advice she gave her students. It's simple, it rings true, and it had never occurred to me before: don't talk about the details of your project while you're working on it. According to Hornik Beer, talking about your current project dissipates the energy, and uses up effort that should be put into writing it.

Sure, you can tell people you're writing a novel or a memoir or whatever. You can even give some general outlines "set in the 1920s" or "based on my mother's journals." But don't let yourself get drawn into discussing the details.

I say this rings true to me because, in my experience, ideas that feel like diamonds in my head seem to hop out of my mouth like a series of warty toads. After all, if you could tell the whole story as well as you can write it, you wouldn't have to write it.

Prompt: The Great Gathering

Assemble everything you know about your project. Once you start, you'll find new ideas being sparked by the old ones. If you don't already, start to carry a notebook around with you so you can jot down ideas as they pass through your brain. You can even get a product called Aquanotes for when you have ideas in the shower!

You might find this the most difficult prompt in *Wording Around with Prose*, because of the sheer mass of material to get down, but doing it will be very rewarding. You can hold in your head the stuff you need for a short poem or story. But a novel, a book-length memoir or travel narrative – for these, you need literary prostheses. How you do it is up to you: sticky notes, or colour-coded recipe cards, or a single document in a word processer, or a database, or the Scrivener app, or a wall with string and sticky notes or recipe cards. Story Grid, the resource for this chapter, may be the answer for some of you.

Resource

Shawn Coyne. *Story Grid.*

Storygrid.com.

Technically, Story Grid is an editing resource. But it is also a good place to get tips on ways of making a useful database for your long writing project. A database is particularly useful if you are thinking of writing a series in the world of your current project. I've given you the website as a resource, but if you prefer, *The Story Grid* is available as a book, and there's a series of five short introductory videos on YouTube.

5. Point of View

Part A: Narrator

How are you going to write this story? Who is your narrator? A character speaking from within the story (first person), or someone looking on from outside of it (third person)?

In First Person Point of View:

- the story is told through the eyes of the narrator using "I"; and
- the narrator is obviously one of the characters.

In *first person limited*, the reader sees what the narrator sees but isn't told what the narrator is thinking.

In *first person omniscient*, the reader sees what the narrator sees and gets inside their head to know what they think.

First person is intimate & compelling; the story unfolds in a suspenseful way because readers go through the events with the narrator. However, it has one important restriction: the audience cannot find out something that the narrator doesn't know, witness, or otherwise find out (they could be told by another character).

Mark Haddon's book *The Curious Incident of the Dog in the Night-Time* is a great example of limited first person point of view. His narrator Christopher is neuroatypical in some unspecified sense; readers learn how Christopher experiences life without the labels that define his barriers. Haddon uses Christopher's observations to reveal things to the audience that Christopher himself cannot understand.

Don't get me started on Stephenie Meyer's Twilight Saga. The third book in that series, *Eclipse,* includes an example of the kinds of problems you can get into with first person narration. In particular, Meyer needs readers to know something that her protagonist Bella can't know, so she has Bella asleep on a sofa while her rival sweethearts Edward and Jake have a long conversation about her. Bella kinda hears it and kinda doesn't. So awkward. So unconvincing.

In Third Person Point of View:

- the story involves characters that the narratorial voice observes and tells readers about, using the pronouns "he, she, they"; and
- the narrator isn't obviously a character in the story.

In *third person limited*, the reader sees everything going on, but has access only to the inner cogitations, the thoughts of one character (usually the protagonist). Sometimes, there's no access to any character's interiority.

In *third person omniscient*, the reader is given insights into the thoughts of many or all the characters.

Third person is the most common point of view because it gives storytellers the most flexibility and freedom. However, it's not as character-driven as a skillfully written first person narration, and so it can be difficult to make it as compelling.

The Harry Potter novels are written in third person: The first time we meet eleven-year-old Harry, we watch him wake up in the cupboard under the stairs. We aren't inside his head, waking up with him.

Second Person

Second Person is the "You" voice. It's very bossy – the voice of things like instruction manuals. Step-by-step instructions have an implied "you" at the beginning of each step. "1. (You) Put tab 'A' into slot 'A'."

In fiction, it's experimental, sometimes used quite successfully. Most writers try to use it at least once, just to see what it's like. My favourite is Italo Calvino's *If on a Winter's Night a Traveler*. Calvino writes:

> In the shop window you have promptly identified the cover with the title you were looking for. Following this visual trail, you have forced your way through the shop past the thick barricade of Books You Haven't Read, which are frowning at you from the tables and shelves, trying to cow you... And thus you pass the outer girdle of ramparts, but then you are attacked by the infantry of Books That If You Had More Than One Life You Would Certainly Also Read But Unfortunately Your Days Are Numbered. With a rapid maneuver you bypass them and move into the phalanxes of the Books You Mean To Read But There Are Others You Must Read First, the Books Too Expensive Now And You'll Wait Till They're Remaindered, the Books Ditto When They Come Out In Paperback, Books You Can Borrow From Somebody, Books That Everybody's Read So It's As If You Had Read Them, Too.

We, the readers, are being told not just that we're looking for a specific book in a bookstore, but also what we're thinking while we're doing it. It's oddly distancing; we're put in the position of object when we're used to being subjects.

A Point of View Cautionary Tale: Harper Lee

Writers sometimes start in one point of view, then realize they can't go on in that one and have to go back and rewrite the whole thing from another point of view. One famous example of this involves Harper Lee's classic *To Kill a Mockingbird*. Published in 1960, it is written in the first person, and won the Pulitzer Prize for Literature in 1961. The only other book published by Lee was *Go Set a Watchman* in 2015 which was, as it turns out, an early draft of *To Kill a Mockingbird. Go Set a Watchman* is written in the third person. It didn't win a Pulitzer. It sold a lot of copies, but that's attributable to Lee's reputation, and because the publisher initially touted it as a sequel to *Kill a Mockingbird* rather than an early draft.

The moral of this story is that you have to be brave. If you've chosen a point of view that just isn't working for you, no matter where you are in the process of writing that first draft – near the beginning, half-way through, or completely finished (like Harper Lee), figure out the better point of view and don't be afraid to start over again.

The Unreliable Narrator

All narrators have agendas; they all have issues that they want to pursue. Thus, to some extent, all narrators are unreliable.

Take, for example, *Wuthering Heights* by Emily Brontë. The narrator of this towering love tale is the namby-pamby Lockwood, who ostensibly tells the story to his housekeeper while she nurses him. Brontë's choice of narrator provides a brilliant contrast between that pair, and the lovers Catherine and Heathcliff. Readers sense that the passion in this story is so extraordinary that it shines through even the dull sensibilities of the narrator and his listener. Also, speaking through Lockwood's voice tames the chaotic passion enough to be told in a story.

Part B: Parataxis and Hypotaxis

Paratactic Storytelling

"Parataxis" is a grammatical term, referring to sequential sentence structure: structures that join clauses, or phrases, or words using conjunctions over and over and over. (See what I did there?) In a paratactic structure, readers get the sense that every element in the list that's been joined together has the same importance as all the others.

In terms of storytelling, parataxis tends to follow a chronological sequence – usually in the third person point of view – wherein the narrator acts like a camera, relating things chronologically. For example, when I boil water, I pour water into a kettle and then put the kettle on the burner, and then turn the burner on its highest setting and then wait until the kettle's whistle tells me the water is boiling. And then I make tea.

Paratactic narratives are common; it's a familiar point of view, largely because we have been trained in this by years of watching movies and television: "this happened, which led to this happening, which led to this..." etc.

Hypotactic (Hierarchical) Storytelling

Technically, "hypotaxis" means the underlying state or underlying substance; the fundamental reality that supports all else. But we're not overly concerned with the philosophy or science of hypotaxis in this book. We want to know why it's a useful concept for storytelling.

In terms of narrative, a hypostatic structure puts the story into the voice of one of the characters, telling it to one of the others.

Why would you do that?

First, *hypostatic storytelling enriches the story*. You, as the author, are not just relating a series of events. It's really about the desires, disappointments, and triumphs of the characters. Putting events into your character's voices lets readers glimpse the fascinating thought processes of those characters. It can help you create sympathy for your characters in your readers' minds.

For example, consider an old, wily lord in his castle, who discovers that one of the strangers who just rode in is his young king and sworn liege, who has barely escaped with his life when his reign was overthrown by a conniving rebel lord. When the king tells that story to the wily old lord, he's going to push a point of view that makes him look as good as he can under the circumstances. On the other hand, the lord's questions are more likely to make the king look unprepared and callow. This nuance would be nigh impossible to convey if the coup and escape were told paratactically as they happened. But telling them in the courtyard of the wily lord's keep makes all sorts of subtleties possible.

Second, *hypotaxis can help you get through long bits quickly*. Instead of having to write two weeks' worth of characters slogging through a swamp, the leader can say "Well, then we slogged through that benighted swamp for two weeks. We donated most of our blood to the blackflies and mosquitos, but the only permanent damage came when Alfie lost his hand to a cottonmouth bite. Swole up big as a cow's head. Feared we'd have to take the whole arm." Bam! Two weeks covered in under 52 words.

Shakespeare uses hypotaxis a lot. For example, *The Winter's Tale* opens with two lords discussing the situation at the court of King Leontes and Queen Hermione, instead of having an act or two full of scenes that show how the situation came to be. So, that's one use of hypotaxis.

Later in *The Winter's Tale*, Leontes' tyrannical paranoia causes him to lose both his daughter and his wife. However, he repents his ways, and in the end, he gets them both back. Now in a paratactic structure, both returning scenes would be shown, one after the other. But a story should have only one climax; two is confusing and not as satisfying. Shakespeare solves this problem by leaving Leontes' reunion with his daughter to occur offstage, described by some secondary characters. This has three important positive implications:

- the meeting with the lost daughter doesn't compete as climax with the meeting with the lost wife;
- the audience is invited to imagine the meeting, which is described in superlative terms (It's good for people to exercise their own imaginations.);

- big scene change can take place behind the stage curtains while having two secondary characters talk in front of the curtains.

Prompt: Revise a section of your story using hypotaxis

Choose a section of your story that you were planning on writing (or have already written) paratactically and rewrite it using hypotaxis. That is to say, have one character tell that bit of the story to another character or set of characters, rather than having the narrator tell the story to readers.

You probably won't find this the most difficult prompt in the book. Maybe you will. Personally, I find rewriting easier than original writing, but I have friends who hate revising and would always rather work on a first draft. So, yeah, maybe you'll find this the most difficult prompt. And the most rewarding!

6. Primary Characters

Part A: The Protagonist

Characters Get Us Started

Often a character, or set of characters, arises first in the author's imagination. They become more and more real and demand that their story be told. They get the narrative ball rolling.

Speaking of reading, in his essay "Fiction and the Figures of Life" William Gass says:

> "We pass most things in novels as we pass things on a train. The words flow by like scenery. All is change. But there are some points in a narrative which remain relatively fixed; we may depart from them, but soon we return, as music returns to its theme. Characters are those primary substances to which everything else is attached." (quoted in Hodgin's *A Passion for Narrative*, 100)

The jury is out on where these imaginary people begin, but they are probably inspired by some synthesis of our own experiences, and by the observations of others, with a smattering of other characters we love added in for spice, all combined through ineffable thing we call imagination. Characters are always some version of Frankenstein's creature made up of bits and pieces with dubious provenance. However, to be convincing, characters need to be consistent, motivated, and plausible (paraphrase of Perrine, also quoted in Hodgins 105).

One Protagonist to Rule Them All

No matter what genre you're working in, your story needs one protagonist. Stories are about individuals, not groups, events, or institutions.

The previous chapter explores some issues about narrators. In a story written in the first person, the narrator may also be the protagonist (i.e. Salinger's *Catcher in the Rye*, Haddon's *Curious Incident of the Dog in the Night-Time.*) Sometimes, the narrator is someone close to the protagonist. In third person, the narrator cannot be the protagonist.

How do You Know Which of Your Characters is the Protagonist?

The protagonist is the character that has the most profound transformation through the course of the novel. Sometimes, an author will realize partway through the writing process – or sometimes very late in the writing process – that the protagonist is actually the person they thought was the sidekick. This realization usually results in a lot of rewriting, and perhaps some private – or not-so-private – profanity.

Some books switch protagonists from chapter to chapter. This a technique can be used to great effect, but it's challenging to maintain. Rick Riordan does it in some of his Heroes of Olympus books, and for my money, the first of those (*The Lost Hero*) is least successful in terms of writing craft. He got better as he did more. If you do want to continually switch protagonists, keep in mind that the protagonist is the character who transforms the most, even if it is only the slight change that can take place within a chapter.

Verisimilitude

In an author's head, the protagonist will be as real as their material-world friends. This is called "verisimilitude" and it applies to all the aspects of a fictional world. If it isn't real to you as the author, it won't be real to your readers.

When I was in high school, Canadian author Margaret Laurence was invited to do a reading in one of my classes. In the Q&A, someone asked what her day looked like when she was working on a novel, and 45 years later, I still remember her answer. She said something along the lines of "I spend the morning with my friends inside my head, and the afternoons with my friends outside it." That's how real her characters had become to her.

Your protagonist needs to feel real to you; they need to evoke feelings from you – compassion, joy, fear, etc. If you empathize with your protagonist, chances are your reader will too.

Narrative Function of the Protagonist

Yes, your protagonist needs to feel real. But no, they aren't real. Often, your protagonist is the threshold, the lens through which your readers come to know the world you are creating. It doesn't matter if you write fiction or creative nonfiction, like memoir or travel writing. Though the protagonist may be a version of you or of someone who actually lived, they are always constructs, made up of the details that you, the author, choose to commit to the page out of the millions of possibilities that don't make it out of your head.

Want, Need, Flaw

At the beginning of your project, your protagonist will have three crucial traits:

A Want

The protagonist's want will be an external, obvious, mission: to get the great McGuffin to the Crack of Doom; to defeat the bully; to escape the tyranny of their mother; to find the perfect shower gift for their brother's fiancée who they think is a terrible person and a dreadful match for their brother; whatever. The protagonist is conscious of the thing that they want.

A Need

Unlike the want, the need is underlying, and internal. Unconscious. Possibly even repressed. However, the protagonist must discover and address the need in order to meaningfully fulfill the want and to set everything right in their life.

At the beginning of the narrative, the protagonist will be unaware of this need; as the story continues, the need surfaces, and the protagonist must confront their need, and then find a way to fulfill it.

Take, for example, the need to find the perfect shower gift for their brother's fiancée who the protagonist actually despises. The author might write events into the story that show how the fiancée reminds the protagonist of their own ex-sweetheart. Once the protagonist realizes that the fiancée isn't the ex, and is in fact a good match for the brother (though not for the protagonist), they will be able to find a gift that will delight the fiancée, because they're then actually buying for the fiancée, and not for the absent ex. That's one way the author could decide to go with that particular want/need situation.

A Flaw

What stops the protagonist from first seeing their need, and then once it is perceived, from fulfilling it? Their flaw. It might be trust – they are too trusting, or too suspicious – it might be pride, it might be self-doubt. In the case of buying the fiancée's shower gift, it's probably grief for their own failed relationship; the protagonist is too wrapped up in their preconceptions about the fiancée to see that they're right for the brother.

Whatever the flaw is, it gets in the way of the protagonist's ability to understand what they need.

What Makes a Tragedy Tragic?

In a comedy or any story with a happy ending, the want is achieved only after recognizing and fulfilling the need, at which point the flaw will be rectified.

Tragedy happens when the protagonist never recognizes their need, only their want, and so achieves neither.

More subtly, tragedy can also happen when the protagonist fulfills their want but never recognizes their need and so their success is hollow. Macbeth becomes king in external ways only; he never understands or achieves the social contract with his thanes to become king in spirit and the result is a great tragedy.

Part B: The Telling Detail

In *A Passion for Narrative* Jack Hodgins' states "…the most vivid characters take on life not so much from an accumulation of information as from the experience of watching this person in action over a number of scenes. And even then, the most memorable characters will sometime leap to life in a single unique and peculiar turn of dialogue" (101). In Chapter 4, I called that the "telling detail." Maurice Shadbolt calls it "a precious particle" (qtd. in Hodgins 101).

What helps us find the telling detail? As with all the things I've talked about in this course, there's no formula, but there are guidelines:

Finding the Right Name

Some people struggle with this. Don't get me started on the ways authors can change and change and change a character's name. If you do that, for the sake of your long-suffering editors, make sure that you do a global search of your document and change all the old names into the one you finally settled on.

Visualization
If you see the character clearly in your own mind, it will be clear in the mind of your readers. Author Jessica Anderson tells the story of seeing a problematic character in her mind as a plumpish blonde. But that character wasn't working out for Anderson. One day, this tall brunette walked into her head and said, "That's me," and from then the character worked (Hodgins 103).

Note on Characters in Creative Nonfiction
Even when we write nonfiction, most stories are character-driven. Of course, creating realistic characters is, in a way, more difficult in creative nonfiction – memoir, travel-writing, etc. – than in fiction. In both genres, characters are constructs; but in creative nonfiction they need to support the illusion of being a historical person. The reader needs to believe not only that the character is real, but also that the character is plausibly the historical person that inspired it.

How is character revealed?
Authors have a lot of options for revealing character, but it boils down to writing down the telling details that you'd notice of actual people. These are some of the clues that reveal character to readers:

- body language;
- emotions (revealed in many ways in the writing: actions, facial expression, verbal or physical diversionary tactics, metaphor, pathetic fallacy, writing style [i.e. repetition, terseness,] etc.);
- dialogue;
- observations (see Hodgins 108-10, Pagh 99-101)

Prompts: Protagonist's Character Questionnaire; Shaped Free Writing on a Primary Character

Appendix 1 is a set of questions to make up a character sheet for your protagonist. Answer all the questions to develop a more fully rounded appreciation of your protagonist. (Hint: if you're reading this in a hard copy, don't scribble your answers down on the page, because you're going to be using the questionnaire again in later chapters).

The prompt for Chapter 1 on Time Management was to do 30 minutes of free writing. This time do at least 30 minutes of almost-free writing. Go longer if you like. Focus on discovering your protagonist or another primary character, considering how that character will cope with the loss of their mentor.

The mentor character may be an actual teacher like Dumbledore, or a wise elder like Gandalf, or a parent, a familiar, perhaps an older sibling or peer of the protagonist. For the protagonist to really develop, they need to learn to think for themselves, and so, at some point in the story, the mentor disappears from the narrative. This forces the protagonist to deal with their loss while coping with the fraught situation driving the plot.

Losing the mentor is a touchstone moment, in which the protagonist becomes real to the reader. We have all lost someone important to us, someone without whom we can't imagine going forward, and yet we must. So, your protagonist's loss will resonate with your readers. *But* this loss needs to be more than the universal expressed personally. What is different, worse, skewed about this loss?

For example, during the COVID isolation in the spring of 2020, my mother-in-law died. Until then, I hadn't realized how much I had learned from her. And because of the isolation, no memorial was possible. All of us who lost her were left alone at a time when company is one of the few balms for coping with such a loss. That isolation was an extraordinary skew to an ordinary sorrow.

(Hint: Your experience, used in either fiction or creative nonfiction projects, adds immeasurably to the sense of truth to the story that you write.)

As with the previous free write, don't stop writing until after the timer rings. If you get stuck, keep repeating the word you just finished until you get unstuck. Lull your internal editor to sleep and let your unconscious drive for a while. You'll be amazed at what falls out of your head when you do.

Resources

Appendix 1's Character Questionnaire, which is based on the sheets given out at a workshop I did with author Bridget Canning at the 2017 FogLit festival in Saint John, New Brunswick, Canada, and from "Ethically Writing Outside Yourself," an interview with Mariam Pirbhai and Waubgeshig Rice, conducted by Sanchari Sur and published in The Writers Union of Canada's *Write* magazine (48.1, Spring 2020).

Jack Hodgins. *A Passion for Narrative: A Guide for Writing Fiction.* McClelland and Stewart, 1993.

Like Pagh's *Write Moves*, *A Passion for Narrative* is a deep writing guide with chapters on all the issues discussed in *Wording Around with Prose*. He is especially cogent on character. Hodgins' book was developed for someone just beginning their prose writing work. The exercises are quite prescriptive; the student isn't likely to be so invested in the material, which means you'll feel freer to make mistakes than if you were working with your own beloved brainchildren.

7. Openings

Raise your hand if you find new books by browsing the shelves of a bookstore or library, opening a book that grabs your attention, and then deciding whether or not to buy or borrow it based on the first few paragraphs. The beginning sentences of your text will take your readers from zero to 100. Other than the title, the cover, and the back blurb – which are pale marketing imitations of the actual writing in your book – the opening hooks readers. There's a reason online booksellers give you the option of downloading the first bit of a text; that's the part that will make or break a sale.

Attributes of a Good Opening

1. The opening will be an image

The opening will be full of action, usually, but that action will be building expectations in the readers' minds, so even the action contributes to building the readers' mental image of the setting, the characters, etc.

2. The opening will set up expectations

If you mislead your reader in the opening, then they will be disappointed later that they didn't get the kind of reading experience they were looking for. If you're writing a zany romantic comedy, the opening should be zany and romantic and comic. If you're writing a multi-generational family tragedy, then the opening should introduce us to at least one tragic member of the family, oppressed by the weight of their relatives' expectations. If it's a cop thriller, the opening should include cops and it should be thrilling. You get the gist.

3. The opening will show the ordinary world

The opening introduces readers to the protagonist's ordinary world. Then it shows how the protagonist's flaw, their need, is ruining every little aspect of their life. For example, in Kinsella's novel *Confessions of a Shopaholic* credit card debt is undermining the security of the protagonist's whole existence. In Tolkien's *The Fellowship of the Ring*, Frodo's near agoraphobic fear of leaving Bag End almost holds him, paralyzed, in Hobbiton. In Mary Shelley's *Frankenstein*, Victor Frankenstein's pride and sense of entitlement lead to tragedy. This hubris is also an attribute of the narrator, the explorer Walton, whose story begins the novel, but Walton learns from Frankenstein's errors and turns back from his noble but doomed voyage.

4. Use the opening to generate empathy for an obnoxious protagonist

If your protagonist's flaw makes them unlikeable in some way, the opening is your chance to create empathy for them. Basically, get your irascible curmudgeon of an antisocial protagonist to save a kitten trapped in a tree (to save the cat, literally) or some other endearing behavior.

Presumably, the protagonist's dislikability will lessen as they transform during the story.

Two Common Problems with Openings

Killing off an early character

Avoid introducing a sympathetic character in the opening of your project, building them up in your readers' minds, then killing them off at the end of the first chapter. All the work you've done creating empathy for that character has to be done all over again. Worse, readers now will be suspicious of you, and it will be harder to get them to trust you again.

Not opening at the beginning of the story
Your narrative should start with the first significant conflict. The story doesn't need to start when the protagonist's day starts. You might not need the first several chapters of set up; go straight to the inciting incident.

The Rule of Exceptions
There are exceptions to everything I've said in this chapter. In fact, there are exceptions to everything I say in this book. If you're going to contravene the conventions, though, you'd better know what you're contravening and have good reasons to do so. That's how you become a skilled writer.

Prompt: Open Your Story to the Reader
Finally, we're getting down to drafting! Maybe you'll find this the most rewarding prompt in the book, though difficult: write, or rewrite, the opening to your project, taking into account the ideas about point of view and character raised thus far. Place the reader by showing what is normal in your protagonists' world, making sure that the reader appreciates that their idea of normal departs from the idea of normal in the protagonist's world, as created by you.

As I hinted in the previous chapter, don't be afraid to draw on extraordinary moments from your lived experience to construct the written world. Even if you're working on memoir, travel writing, or some other form of creative nonfiction, you are constructing the world. For example, in June 2020, I took my dog along a deserted trail and found myself running through a cloud of monarch butterflies flocked on a debris of stinky red shells – the remains of a lobster feast, dumped in front of a bear blind. I guess shutting down North America meant that more monarchs survived their multi-generation migration to Canada. This might provide an image that I'd try out as the opening to a story or novel – beautiful, tough butterflies thick on carrion that had been dumped to attract predators and make them easier to hunt.

Final bit of advice for this prompt: don't stress over your opening the first few times you revise it, but also, don't stress over having to revise it a lot. The opening has to be the best writing in the book.

Resource

Jessica Brody. *Save the Cat! Writes a Novel: The Last Book on Novel Writing You'll Ever Need.* Ten Speed Press, 2018.

Brody's book includes useful ideas about protagonists, openings, and structure. Brody organizes the genres by the type of transformation that the protagonist goes through. Personally, I'm not enamored with Brody's writing style but the content is good.

8. Plot and Structure

"'The king died and then the queen died' is a story.
'The king died, and then queen died of grief' is a plot."
– EM Forster, *Aspects of the Novel*

Part A: Plot

Compounding Conflict

According to Forster, story is what happens; plot is story (what happens) *plus* motivation: the king died and, as a result, the queen died of grief. The death of the king was the inciting incident of the death of the queen.

That's what "compounding conflict" means. Things don't happen randomly or coincidentally in a plot, the way they tend to in real life. Authors have multiple reasons for structuring each detail into a story, no matter what the conventions of that plot are (See Appendix 2 for Booker's list of Seven Basic Plots.) Bits of information and action that you seed into your story early should become significant later.

Furthermore, determining the sequence of revelation (the order in which plot elements and other aspects of the narrative arise) is one of the most difficult things for an author to learn. In Part B of Chapter 5, we covered Hypotaxis, or telling part of the story by having a character relay it to another character, after the fact (rather than having the omniscient narrator relay it as it is ongoing). *That* is a structural decision.

Part B: Structure

Structure is: what happens (story), plus motivation (plot), consciously presented in a sequence that hooks the reader into continuing to read.

Creating Structure: Plotters and Pantsers (or Plantsers, or Potters…)

Your writing habits probably put you somewhere on the continuum between plotter or a pantser.

- A *plotter* is someone who plots the whole story out carefully before beginning;
- A *pantser* is someone who writes by the seat of their pants, going where inspiration takes them, also known as a *discovery writer.*

Most writers are not wholly one or the other but write by some combination of discovery and plotting.

Problems? Plotters can easily morph into plodders. If you map out your story and then follow your outline slavishly, always colouring inside the lines as it were, you're likely to work quickly but get bored. If you, the author, are bored while writing, that boredom will be communicated to your readers.

On the other hand, pantsers are far more likely to "write themselves into a corner" – discover halfway through that they should have chosen third person instead of first, or that the sidekick – or worse, the antagonist – is actually their protagonist. For example, think of *Paradise Lost*: Lucifer starts out sitting at the right hand of God, suffers a week-long fall into the lake of fire from which he arises saying "Evil be thou my good." It's hard to imagine a more extreme transformation. That's why, for centuries people have argued that the antagonist – Satan – is really the protagonist of *Paradise Lost.*

Structure, Script and Screenwriting

Performance genres of writing are a great way to learn structure. They need to have strong structures because, in order to be produced, a lot of people have to understand the very bones of what is going on. Performances are essentially collaborative. Movies, for example, tend to be structured in predictable ways. Sometimes the result is a magnificent piece of art that shows how capable of glory the human imagination really is. Most movies are not that, alas.

Artists' Parallax Vision

It's time to bring to the fore, gentle authorial readers, a binary underlying all of these lessons. In each, we discuss the text on the level of the story – the pseudo-lived experience that the reader will enjoy. But as authors, we also talk about the structure, the creation of which is concurrent with and integral to the story. Writing is like ballet or cooking, painting or – let's face it – all of the creative arts; done well it looks easy, but for most of us, getting to that ease means thousands of hours of hard work.

Don't Get Me Started on the Apparent Ease of Creative Work

The apparent ease of sophisticated creative production is, I think, why arts are undervalued in our Western world; done well, something creative looks easy. Done poorly – by people still working towards mastery – it gets dismissed as bad. Instead of being understood as a point on a developing continuum of imaginative exploration and learning, our impatient culture judges and moves on. It's a sadly impoverished way of looking at the world.

For example, my friend Roland Daigle published a graphic novel called *Alerte a Richibuctou* in 2019. I know that there are some single frames in that work that he spent two weeks drawing. Most readers will not spend two minutes looking at them. Why? Because they are successful; they advance the story without making you aware of the craft.

Many writers early in their careers are tricked by that apparent ease. Reading is easy. Writing – though immense fun – always demands more of you as an author. I hate to be the one to tell you this, but in my experience, writing well doesn't get easier the more you do it; the problems you tackle just get more and more sophisticated as you improve as a writer. Maurice Blanchot understood that when he penned *The Writing of the Disaster.* To him, writing is like digging; you're trying to get yourself out of a hole by digging deeper in.

Artists' Parallax Vision, redux

As an author you create a kind of double-vision for yourself. There's the verisimilitude – the world-building that persuades the reader to suspend their disbelief and go where you take them in your story, whatever genre it is. Then there's the created-ness, the craft that you carefully structure into your project. That craft carries your readers to the place of suspended disbelief. If you write well, the craft will be invisible to your reader. However, the craft has to be real and important to you, the author. That's the huge gulf between the reader's experience and the writer's experience.

Structuring Conventions

Let's be clear here; following convention doesn't need to result in formulaic writing. As I noted in Chapter 3, it takes three ingredients – five if you're lucky to have them – to make bread, but there are a million million different kinds of bread out there. Similarly, plots may be conventional but there's a million million variations possible within those conventions – in writing style, character, setting, conflict, point of view, structure, and all the aspects of the craft of writing.

The following are some common structuring conventions.

The Three Act Structure, Freytag's Model, Time Clock
Two of the most prevalent ways of modeling story structure are often built into the same movie scripts:

- *Three acts*: 1. Intro (20%ish), 2. Rising action (70%ish), 3. Climax & Resolution (10%ish)
- *Freytag's 19th Century pyramidal shape of five steps*; 1. Exposition, 2. Rising Action (including the nadir), 3. Climax, 4. Falling Action, and 5. Resolution

Along with the combination of those two models, you usually find a thing called "Time Clock." About two-thirds of the way through the narrative, something happens to increase the urgency, at the fulcrum between the second and third acts. This moment is usually the nadir, the low point, for the protagonist, Often it's a failure brought about by their obliviousness to their need. It makes their flaw obvious. Because of this low point, they discover their need, recognize their flaw, and complete their transformation into the character who can triumph in the climax.

The most obvious example of "Time Clock" occurs in kidnapping stories; the first attempt to drop off the ransom is always bungled. Suddenly the victim's life is even more at risk. We discover they're in some kind of trap that will kill them if the heroes don't get to them in x number of hours. That ratcheted-up tension is a result of the time-clock.

Three Potential Structuring Models: The Hero's Journey, The Heroine's Journey, and The Virgin's Promise
More recent narrative structuring models are based on the idea of "beats" – not shaggy poets, but plot points that an author should hit to make it more likely that you will succeed in your storytelling. A *beatsheet* is a map of a story's plot points. Different genres demand that the author hit different beats. Beatsheets aren't formulae that some egghead made up and

imposed on authors who must follow them slavishly. Different beatsheets for different genres arose from smart people who had read very widely in the genre noticing the most successful texts tend to cover similar points in similar sequences. Then they kindly wrote them down and made it possible for the rest of us to benefit from their observations.

One of the first books to map out a story's plot points is Christopher Vogler's *Writer's Journey: Mythic Structure for Storytellers and Screenwriters* (1985). Vogler based his beatsheet on Joseph Campbell's "Hero's Journey" in *The Hero with a Thousand Faces* (1949). Texts that follow this beatsheet include *The Lord of the Rings*, *The Odyssey,* and *Guardians of the Galaxy.* The Hero's Journey's beatsheet looks like this:

1. Ordinary World
2. Call to Adventure
3. Refusal of the Call
4. Meeting with the Guide
5. Crossing the First Threshold
6. Tests, Allies, Enemies
7. Approach to the Inmost Cave (the Lair of the Enemy)
8. Crisis/Nadir
9. Rewarded
10. Road Back
11. Final Battle
12. Return with the Elixir.

Vogler's source – Joseph Campbell's *Hero's Journey*– was a product of his time and doesn't interrogate its own patriarchalism. So Vogler's model reifies only one type of heroic story, at the expense of all the others.

In 1990, when women-centered approaches were becoming widely accepted in the popular imagination, Maureen Murdock wrote a beatsheet which she calls *The Heroine's Journey: Woman's Quest for Wholeness*. DC's *Wonder Woman* stories tend to follow this beatsheet.

1. Heroine separates from the feminine
2. Identification with the masculine and gathering of allies
3. Road or trials and meeting ogres and dragons.
4. Experiencing the boon of success
5. Heroine awakens to feelings of spiritual aridity / death
6. Initiation and descent to the goddess.
7. Heroine urgently yearns to reconnect with the feminine
8. Heroine heals the mother / daughter split
9. Heroine heals the wounded masculine within
10. Heroine integrates the masculine and feminine.

More recently, some authors have felt that between them Vogler and Murdock reinscribe gender as a binary that undervalues other ways of looking at story. Thus, Kim Hudson came out with *The Virgin's Promise* (2009). Texts that follow this beatsheet include *Cinderella*, *While You Were Sleeping*, and *Frozen*. In The Virgin's Promise, the protagonist

1. lives in a dependent world, and so
2. pays the price of conformity, until they are given
3. an opportunity to shine, for which they
4. dress the part. They thus come to know a
5. secret world and
6. no longer fit in their dependent world. Eventually they are
7. caught shining, and have to
8. give up what keeps them stuck. This throws the
9. kingdom into chaos, while the protagonist
10. wanders in the wilderness. Eventually, she
11. chooses her light, which leads to
12. the re-ordering which results in
13. the kingdom becoming brighter.

A quick online search will uncover beatsheets for many other genre-based narrative structures. Go to the search engine of your choice, type in the genre name and "beatsheet," and see what comes up. For example, for romances, have a look at Gwen Hayes' *Romancing the Beat* (2016). Hayes' table of contents gives you the beats.

Prompt: Work Out Beats

This is a three-part prompt.

1. Choose a favourite story in the genre of your project. Find a beatsheet for the genre to figure out the beats (significant plot points) in that favourite story.

2. Use what you've learned in this chapter and in part one of this prompt to map out the beats in your own project. You can use the beatsheet you chose for part one here, or another one, or you can just wing it.

3. Play around with the beats in your story – adding some, removing others, changing the sequence – to create the most effective, dramatic, and dynamic structure possible.

Figuring out the beats in your own work is the most difficult prompt I've asked of you, so doing it first for an existing story by someone else will reward you by helping to get the structural ideas into your brain and bones before you attempt it in your own project.

Resources

Zach Bohannon and J. Thorn. "The Three Story Method Influencer Series." *The Career Author Podcast,* episodes 111-115, February-March 2020, thecareerauthor.com/podcast/.

These podcast episodes introduce several ways of structuring a story: #111- Aristotle, #112-Hero's Journey, #113-Virgin's Promise, #114-McKee's Story, and #115 The Three Story Method. The discussion of structures usually doesn't get rolling until about the twentieth minute. You can also look at the websites of the beatsheets given above. Finally, Story Grid (resource for Chapter 4) will also be helpful in finding beatsheets and working out the beats.

9. Secondary Characters

Part A: Types

Character Equals Desire

Nancy Pagh suggests that it helps to think of a character as "essentially a desire, or yearning, represented as a specific person.... Desiring revenge, Ahab sets off in the wake of Moby Dick. Desiring passion, Madame Bovary chases her romantic fantasy. Desiring wisdom, Doctor Faustus makes a deal with the devil" (Pagh 95).

Hierarchy of Characters

Not all characters are created equal.

- *Primary*: The main characters, without whom the narrative cannot exist. The reader should have a strong emotional response to the primary characters.
- *Secondary*: Still important, but more for keeping things moving in the story. They usually evoke less emotion in readers than the primary characters.
- *Others*: These characters are often unnamed. They serve a narrative function, but too much detail about them distracts from the main story.

Don't include extra characters in your story; two flat, *secondary* or *other* characters may work better as one, slightly more complex character.

Traditional Story Characters

Most stories will have these:

- Protagonist: Want, need, flaw: the character who transforms the most. (Caveat: In Gwen Hayes's *Romancing the Beat*, she talks about Hero 1 & Hero 2, which is the only place I've found that contravenes the "one protagonist per story" rule. Just more evidence that you need to deeply understand the conventions of your genre.)
- *Antagonist*: Similar traits to the Protagonist – want, need, flaw, but their desires are inimical to the Protagonist's. Also, the antagonist rarely recognizes their need, let alone achieves it; they are resigned to living with their flaws. This is a crucial difference from the Protagonist.
- *Beloved*: If the plot is flagging, put the beloved in danger.
- *Sidekick (Buddy)*: If the beloved is formidable, a handy sidekick can be imperiled (i.e. Willow in the early seasons of *Buffy the Vampire Slayer*).

Archetypes (Jungian)

The early days of psychoanalysis may have led to dodgy, context-mired counselling practices, but folks like Freud and Jung, and later Campbell (*Hero with a Thousand Faces*) were excellent storytellers. Jung's archetypes in particular have proven useful to authors in the century since he delineated them.

Even though your characters should feel real to you in order to feel real to the readers, many of them will also serve a symbolic function. Readers may not be fully conscious of this symbolic function, but it will make the reading experience much richer. Some archetypes are:

- Hero
- Mentor (wise guide)
- Threshold Guardian (Charon, executive assistant, etc.)

- Herald (knight's squire, pilot fish, telephone's ring)
- Shapeshifter (a character of ambigous alignment)
- Shadow (a pale imitation of the protagonist, helpless before their flaw)
- Trickster (marches to the pound of a distant plumber; disdainful of other's passions, fears).

Caveat on Stereotypes

Don't get me started on stereotypes or oversimplified characters which reinforce a shallow yet widely-held view of people who live with a certain trait or set of circumstances. Stereotypes reinforce prejudices. As an author, you need to take care that your enthusiasm over the symbolic function of a character doesn't blind you to their dependence on stereotypes.

Part B: Diversity

Miriam Pirbhai and Waubgeshig Rice, when interviewed by Sanchari Sur, suggested that authors approach writing diversity with the following three questions in mind:

1. Why are you drawn to this character? (Or how does your interest in this story / character relate to your own practices as a storyteller?)
2. What about this story / character draws you?
3. How complex is your understanding of the character / story? (Sur 11)

Ever since the 1970s, there has been growing contention about writing characters who are not like the author. Writers walk a fine line between developing respectful, under-represented characters and appropriating someone else's identity and culture. Ignorance feeds appropriation as a means of perpetuating stereotypes – a poorly-written character, can harmfully misrepresent a population that the author is not. Stories have the power to change minds and influence actions, and authors need to understand what kinds of changes they want their stories to instigate.

There's not enough diversity in Western literature. We need more representation for LGBTQIA2S+ identities, people who are differently abled or have disabilities, BIPOC, people from diverse cultural backgrounds, neurodivergent individuals, and more. The stories of many astonishing people remains marginalized.

Live with your characters. Have coffee with them. Go for walks with them. Learn their joys and sorrows and phobias. And do research.

Prompt: Get to Know Your Characters & Draft with Diversity

Do Appendix 1's Character Questionnaire (first used in the prompt for Chapter 6) to work up character details for your antagonist, sidekick(s), love interests, and/or other characters. This is not the most difficult prompt in *Wording Around with Prose* (whew!), though you might find it the most rewarding. The three questions proposed by Pirbhai and Rice have been integrated into Appendix 1. Keep drafting your story, with an eye to expanding and questioning the diversity of your characters and keeping an eye on the macro/micro relationships.

Your story should be about things that matter, and as such, it is going to be impacted by important events. Maybe your plot involves the protagonist interacting with the Great and Powerful of the world you've created. Maybe the relationship between your fictional world's politics and the characters you depict are not so direct. Even so, you need to be very clear about the political structure of your creation, and how it impacts your characters. Frankly, nothing could provide more diverse, dramatic, life-and-death models for your created world than the political and social realities rendered in the COVID-19 crucible of spring 2020.

Resources

Christopher Vogler. *The Writer's Journey: Mythic Structure for Storytellers and Screenwriters.* Michael Weise Productions, 1985.

I've mentioned Vogler's text several times prior to this chapter, but it is particularly relevant here as the source for the discussion of Jungian archetypes, and the "Journey of the Hero" beatsheet. This chapter also draws heavily on Pagh's *Write Moves* (resource for Chapter 2).

Francina Simone. "How to Write Diverse Characters | NaNoWriMo." *YouTube,* 5 Feb 2019,

Simone provides an alternative point of view to that of Pirbhai and Rice. This video is only seven minutes long, quite controversial, and full of swearing. Simone concludes "Do the best you can do, do good, and flourish."

10. Conflict

Conflict is hard

The sixth of Kurt Vonnegut's *8 Basics of Creative Writing 101* is "Be a sadist. No matter how sweet and innocent your leading characters, make awful things happen to them—in order that the reader may see what they are made of" (see appendix 2). This is difficult. As writers, our characters should be people we would want as friends, and we want our friends to have easy, stress-free lives. But that makes for boring stories. Instead, we need to strew our characters' lives with the caltrops of conflict. We need to put them through h-e-double-hockey-sticks.

Conflict is between characters

Characters have conflicting wants and needs.

I use the term "character" loosely; it could be another human, it could be an animal, it could be an object. In some cases the very setting becomes a character who opposes the protagonist.

Things can't go easily for your protagonist; personalities will clash, good characters will misunderstand each other, and evil characters will sew dissent among the good.

Conflict needs to feel organic, not contrived

Create clever, believable conflict. Sometimes, I run into texts where the conflicts seem manufactured for the sake of the plot, or because the author is slavishly following a beatsheet. They read "the protagonist and the love interest must misunderstand each other," and they drop a stupid argument in. I find it difficult to stay engaged if the conflict doesn't feel real.

For example, in Lucy Maude Montgomery's *The Blue Castle* (which is a guilty pleasure book for me), the protagonist Valancy gets a terrible shock that should have killed her, given her heart condition. But it doesn't. Her husband runs away because, she thinks, he realizes that he's stuck with her for the rest of their days. In fact, he ran because he couldn't stand the thought of losing her. Complete misunderstanding between the two, but even when I first read this at twelve years old, I didn't find his decamping believable.

Boring moments are moments without conflict

If you have a section in your story without conflict, ask yourself: "Is this section really necessary?" It probably isn't. You can probably drop that scene's *raison d'etre* into another scene, and simply cut this one.

If, however, you think you can't get away with cutting it, look for wishy-washy words or phrases like "tried," "wished," "lost their nerve," "wanted," etc. They might indicate a character making a bland choice. Rewrite the scene such that the character makes a bad decision and conflict results.

Prompt: Continue to Draft Your Project

Keep drafting your project, keeping in mind the conflicts. Are they plausible? Are they dramatic? Are you putting your beloved characters through sufficient pain and difficulty?

You've probably figured out by now that I feel like whatever you're currently working on is the most difficult part of writing. It's also the most rewarding because you are going forward with your project. You're not just improving as a writer; you're improving as a thinker. The better we are at using language, the better we think.

Resource

Kurt Vonnegut's "Creative Writing 101"

From the Introduction to Vonnegut's *Bagombo Snuff Box* (G. P. Putnam's Sons, 1999):

1. Use the time of a total stranger in such a way that he or she will not feel the time was wasted.
2. Give the reader at least one character he or she can root for.
3. Every character should want something, even if it is only a glass of water.
4. Every sentence must do one of two things—reveal character or advance the action.
5. Start as close to the end as possible.
6. Be a sadist. No matter how sweet and innocent your leading characters, make awful things happen to them—in order that the reader may see what they are made of.
7. Write to please just one person. If you open a window and make love to the world, so to speak, your story will get pneumonia.
8. Give your readers as much information as possible as soon as possible. To heck with suspense. Readers should have such complete understanding of what is going on, where and why, that they could finish the story themselves, should cockroaches eat the last few pages.

The greatest American short story writer of my generation was Flannery O'Connor (1925-1964). She broke practically every one of my rules but the first. Great writers tend to do that. (Vonnegut 12)

11. Setting

One important teacher in my life was Dr. Peter Schwenger in the English Department at Mount Saint Vincent University in Halifax, where I did my undergraduate BA back in the early nineties. He wrote a book called *Fantasm & Fiction: On Textual Envisioning* which marvels at how we create pictures in our minds simply by reading words. Truly, it's one of those everyday mysteries that we accept without thought most of the time.

In the opening pages, Schwenger recounts how he got a "B" "for Bemused perhaps" on the first essay he wrote for his first undergrad English class. The essay was on Jane Austen's *Emma*, and he concluded his essay

> with an analysis of the scene in which the loathesome Mr. Elton proposes to Emma during a carriage ride through a wintry night. I dwelt on the ways that the mental agitation of the scene is mirrored by its physical qualities: the dash of snow against the carriage windows; the jolting of the carriage on the uneven road; the fitful illumination of the carriage lamps, catching at intervals the violet silk lining of Emma's bonnet (1).

Of course, those of you who know *Emma* realize that there is no such scene.

We could merely chalk this up to another undergrad trying to disguise poor reading – or no reading – with good prose… but in *Fantasm & Fiction,* Schwenger protests that he *did* read the book, and something else was going on. Something about Austen's prose, some magical combination of details, provided the spark that made the entire scene rise up in his imagination such that he, to use his own words, "entered the text" (1). He points out that, though this is an extreme example, it's something that happens every time we read imaginative work. The number of details on the page is miniscule in comparison with the images that arise in our minds when we read. Furthermore, hose images are not usually as complete as we believe – they tend to devolve into a sort of fog around the edges until we put our attention on them.

Those minimal particulars that lead readers, all unwitting, to create a complex mental image are what I call "telling details." It's true of character, and it's true of setting. When you put the right details in the right order, the whole scene will spark into life. In fact, Nancy Pagh sees character and setting as so similar that she puts them in the same chapter in her book *Write Moves*. Pagh is a good resource on setting, as is Hodgins. But for the balance of this chapter, I use Robert McKee's book *Story: Substance, Structure, Style and the Principles of Screenwriting.* (I am not using Schwenger's *Fantasm & Fiction* because it's a very academic and theoretical text, which isn't the focus of this book.)

Remember way back to the discussion of structure, when I said that we who write prose can learn a lot about structure by studying and writing scripts? Well, McKee's book is a case in point.

Avoiding Clichés

In his chapter called "Structure and Setting," McKee notes that setting profoundly affects what can happen in your story; it sharply defines and confines the possibilities (69). McKee calls this "Creative Limitation" and affirms that a writer needs to know their world thoroughly. Most of what authors know about their worlds doesn't make it to the final draft, but skimping on world building leads to clichéd settings and characters. Don't get me started on clichés. They are the stereotypes of language. George Elliott Clarke (more on him in the next chapter) calls clichés "dead language."

So how do you avoid clichés? Do all sorts of research and pre-writing, as I introduced in chapters 3 and 4.

McKee's Delineation of Settings

McKee asserts that setting has three dimensions (68-69):

1. Geographical setting.

When we first think about setting, we usually assume that means geography.

1a. *Overarching* – a country, a city, a set of intersecting cultures, geographies. For example, on Fredericton's southside, you'll find two universities, the provincial legislature, an oddly stellar public art gallery, various markets, a commercial district, the Stepping Stone Seniors Centre, the Victoria Health Centre, the Community Kitchen, and several shelters, all within a few minutes' walk of each other. Even though Fredericton is a small, weirdly homogenized city, there's a diverse variety of settings available.

1b. *Specific* – individual rooms in specific buildings, defined external spaces – not just Wilmot Park, but the bench in the gazebo in Wilmot Park.

2. Temporal setting

2a. *Period* – your story's place in time (Contemporary, the 1960s, Victorian, near future, far future, etc.)

2b. *Duration* – the length of time covered in the story.

3. Social setting

McKee calls it "Level of Conflict," which is the human dimension: "the political, economic, ideological, biological and psychological forces of society shape events as much as period, landscape or costume" (McKee 69). Conflict doesn't merely arise between characters; it's inherent in setting, as well.

McKee suggests social setting is fundamentally hierarchical, based on the level of conflict. As the author you need to know if your story's focus is on the protagonist's:

- inner (possibly unconscious) conflicts, or
- conflicts with other individuals, or
- conflicts with social institutions, and/or situations.

Back in the bad old days when I was a high school student, I learned this as: man vs himself, man vs man, man vs nature. Socially, we've come a distance since then!

To me, social setting is the setting of the society in which the story operates: class, race, gender, sexuality, etc. Social setting is strongly related to geographical and temporal settings. For example, in Fredericton during the COVID-19 isolation in the spring of 2020, Fredericton High School was used as a shelter for homeless people. Everyone got their own room. Interviewed on the radio, one man said he hadn't slept so well in years. So that situation depends upon all three of McKee's sources of conflict: location (Fredericton High School), time (spring 2020), and social (homeless people in a relatively upscale locale). This is an intersection of settings chock full of possibilities for dramatic conflict.

Prompt: Treat Your Setting as a Character

One final time, do the character questionnaire in Appendix 1, but this time treat your primary settings as characters. It will require you to use your imagination. You've got this.

Blah, blah, most difficult, blah, blah, rewarding, blah.

Resource

Robert McKee. *Story: Substance, Structure, Style, and the Principles of Screenwriting*. HarperCollins, 1997.

12. Dialogue

It takes time and patience to develop skill at writing dialogue. Trouble writing dialogue usually stems from one of two problems:

- Lack of verisimilitude: if the characters don't feel real to you, then their speech acts aren't going to feel real either. (Note: every line of dialogue will be an act done in speech. There's no filler; each speech should serve multiple functions in your story: revealing character, forwarding the plot, planting important information for the compounding conflict, etc.).
- Over-writing: people don't talk in full, grammatically correct sentences, so your dialogue shouldn't consist of full, grammatically correct sentence either.

Both of these problems can be alleviated by writing more dialogue and always reading your dialogue aloud. In fact, you should always read everything you write aloud.

Eavesdropping will help too.

One Recommendation

In 2006, I attended a workshop led by George Elliott Clarke who went on to become the Poet Laureate of Toronto, and later the Poet Laureate of Canada. His advice for developing a better ear for dialogue is to eavesdrop. Always carry a little book around with you to jot down what you hear.

Don't wait to write down what you hear; do it as soon as you hear it, or as soon as possible after. If you wait, you will "remember" your own words and phrasing, not what was actually said. A big part of the point of eavesdropping is to get a sense of cadence, lilt, vocabulary, and phrasing which is not naturally your own.

If you write things down immediately, you'll be surprised by how clear the meaning of people's speech is, despite how little they actually say.

This recommendation is about practice, not ethics. You need to come to your own peace with the ethics of eavesdropping.

One Caveat

Eavesdropping on scripted conversations – on television, in movies, in audiobooks, etc. – doesn't count; they've already been formed by someone else's creative aesthetic. If you're studying those things, you're studying those authors' craft, which has value, but it isn't the value of eavesdropping.

Prompt: Writing Talking

1. Go somewhere with lots of people talking informally (a food court, a movie theatre, a café or restaurant, a hospital cafeteria, an arena or stadium etc.), and write down what you hear people say.
2. Look at the speech acts you eavesdropped on. Do any of them sound like something one of your characters would say? Revise one or more of them so that they fit in your character's mouth and then write dialogue with another character using what you've learned.

Resources

Here I've focused on only one method for improving dialogue – eavesdropping – but any good general source on writing craft will have a chapter on writing dialogue.

If you want to go more deeply on this topic, dig out your copy of Pagh's *Write Moves*, or Hodgins's *A Passion for Narrative*, or McKee's *Story*, all of which were the resources mentioned in other chapters.

Conclusion: The Story So Far

I wish I could say, "Ta Da! You've worked all the way through *Wording Around with Prose*, so you must have a solid first draft of your project in front of you." Unfortunately, writing doesn't work like that. *Wording Around with Prose* has, at least, touched on the most important aspects involved in the craft of writing prose (I think. [Probably. {Most of them anyway.}]). I hope it has done so in a manner that both excites you to continue with your project and reassures you that your project can, in fact, be finished soon.

As noted in the prompt to Chapter 10, all the prompts are "the most difficult" because the writing you're doing right now is what's making you sweat blood, no matter what it is. Most of us started writing because we love reading. But writing has the same relationship to reading that dancing the dying swan has to sitting in the audience and watching Swan Lake. The latter is easy and makes few demands on us. The former, however, succeeds only if we work hard, if we work intelligently, and if we continually practice to improve our craft. And the person in the audience, while they may appreciate and be moved by the dance, will never feel the joy of doing it themselves and getting it right.

Here's a reflection from student Denise McClure about working through Wording Around with Prose: "It was … motivating and encouraging, and yes, I hit a bit of frustration… the assignments put me in some tough spots and helped me out of them – which, I believe, is the goal as I move forward: growth."

Through all this difficulty, though, there is bliss in seeing our ephemeral ideas take form outside of our skulls in a manuscript, and eventually, a book that can be shared with people we haven't even met. I hope that *Wording Around with Prose* has helped you get closer to that goal.

Prompt: Get to the end of the first draft

Keep working on the first draft until it's all out of your head and onto the page.

List of Prompts

1. Free Write for 30 Minutes (Prepping)
2. Find a Way to Fit Writing into Your Life (Time Management)
3. Research Your Genre (Understanding Genre)
4. The Great Gathering (Organizing)
5. Revise a Section of Your Story Using Hypotaxis (Narration)
6. Protagonist's Character Questionnaire; Shaped Free Writing on a Primary Character (Character Development)
7. Open Your Story to the Reader (Beginnings)
8. Work Out Beats (Structure)
9. Get to Know Your Characters & Draft with Diversity (Character Development)
10. Continue to Draft Your Project (Conflict)
11. Treat Your Setting as a Character (Setting)
12. Writing Talking (Dialogue)
13. Get to the End of the First Draft (Completing)

Suggested Resources

Chapter 1. "NaNo Prep 101 Workshop." *NaNoWriMo,* preview.nanowrimo.org/nano-prep-101. Accessed April 2020.

Chapter 2. Nancy Pagh. *Write Moves: A Creative Writing Guide and Anthology*. Broadview Press, 2016.

Chapter 3. A writing book specific to your genre (i.e. Gwen Hayes' *Romancing the Beat*, Stephen King's *On Writing,* Dianna Wynne Jones's *Tough Guide to Fantasyland,* etc.).

Chapter 4. Shawn Coyne. *Story Grid*. Storygrid.com. Accessed May 2020.

Chapter 5. No resource given. Any writing book worth its salt will provide advice on narration.

Chapter 6. Character Questionnaire (Appendix 1); Jack Hodgins. *A Passion for Narrative: A Guide for Writing Fiction*. McClelland and Stewart, 1993.

Chapter 7. Jessica Brody. *Save the Cat! Writes a Novel: The Last Book on Novel Writing You'll Ever Need.* Ten Speed Press, 2018.

Chapter 8. Zach Bohannon and J. Thorn. "The Three Story Method Influencer Series." *The Career Author Podcast,* episodes 111-115, February-March 2020, thecareerauthor.com/podcast/.

Chapter 9. Christopher Vogler. *The Writer's Journey: Mythic Structure for Storytellers and Screenwriters*. Micheal Weise Productions, 1985; Francina Simone. "How to Write Diverse Characters | NaNoWriMo." *YouTube,* 5 Feb 2019, youtu.be/9qYsBwfrojQ.

Chapter 10. Kurt Vonnegut. “Creative Writing 101.” From the Introduction to *Bagombo Snuff Box.* G. P. Putnam’s Sons, 1999.

Chapter 11. Robert McKee, *Story: Substance, Structure, Style, and the Principles of Screenwriting*. HarperCollins, 1997.

Chapter 12. Pagh (Chapter 2), Hodgins (Chapter 6), and McKee (Chapter 11), yet again.

Appendix 1: Character Questionnaire

Character Basics

1. What do you think the character wants more than anything?
2. What do you think the character needs more than anything?
3. What do you think is the character's flaw (fatal flaw, besetting sin, biggest problem, etc.)?

Things the Author Should Know

Adapted from Bridget Canning's
Character Development Workshop,
FogLit Festival, Saint John NB Canada, Sept 3—2017.

1. Age______ Gender_________________
2. Names____
3. Eye Colour___________ Hair (Colour, Style)__________________________
4. Most striking or memorable physical feature.
5. Characteristics/Mannerisms.
6. Describe their speaking voice, and likely vocabulary.
7. How does the character feel in their body?
8. Sum this person up in one word.
9. What are the character's emotional strengths?
10. What are the character's emotional weaknesses?
11. What is one thing this person can do very well?
12. What is one thing this person does not do well?
13. What is the character wearing? Do they like their clothes? Is there anything special about them?
14. What is in their pockets?
15. Compare this character to a door.

Things to Think About to Deepen Diversities in Your Story/Character

Adapted from "Ethically Writing Outside Yourself," an interview with Mariam Pirbhai and Waubgeshig Rice conducted by Sanchari Sur, in The Writers Union of Canada's *Write* magazine (48.1, Spring 2020).

1.Why are you drawn to this character? (Or, how does your interest in this story / character relate to your own practices as a storyteller?)
2. What about this story / character draws you?
3. How complex is your understanding of the character / story?

Appendix 2: Seven Basic Plots

(from Christopher Booker's *The Seven Basic Plots)*

There are many lists of basic plots out there. Christopher Booker's list is the most familiar one to most of us:

1. Overcoming the Monster (*Beowulf, Buffy the Vampire Slayer*).
2. Rags to Riches (*Orphan Annie*, *Twilight*).
3. The Quest (*The Lord of the Rings, The Odyssey*).
4. Voyage and Return (*The Iliad*, *Voyage of the Dawn Treader*, *Outlander*).
5. Comedy (*The Guernsey Literary and Potato Peel Pie Society*). Note: Romance is a subgenre of Comedy.
6. Tragedy (*Macbeth, Beowulf*). Note: Tragedy is the flip side of the *Overcoming the Monster* plot. So, when Beowulf-as-hero confronts and vanquishes Grendel, and later Grendel's mother, the plot is Overcoming the Monster. More subtly, when Beowulf-as-king confronts and vanquishes the dragon, the genre is Tragedy. Kings should send young heroes on quests; it is not a king's job to undertake a quest himself.
7. Rebirth (*A Christmas Carol*). Note: as with the *Tragedy* plot, but the protagonist realizes their error just before it's too late and transforms. "Rebirth" is sometimes positioned as a subgenre of comedy.

Works and Authors Cited, by Chapter

Chapter 1

"NaNo Prep 101 Workshop." *NaNoWriMo,* 2020, preview.nanowrimo.org/nano-prep-101.

Chapter 2

Grey, Zane.

"Killing it on Kickstarter with Russell Nohelty." *Stark Reflections on Writing and Publishing,* 21 Aug 2020, starkreflections.ca/2020/08/21/episode-149-killing-it-on-kickstarter-with-russell-nohelty.

Pagh, Nancy. *Write Moves: A Creative Writing Guide and Anthology.* Broadview Press, 2016.

Robinson, Eden. *Son of a Trickster.* Knopf Canada, 2017.

Chapter 3

Arcudi, John, and Doug Mahnke, creators. *The Mask.* Dark Horse Comics, 1991.

Grossman, Lev. *The Magicians.* Viking, 2009.

Hayes, Gwen. *Romancing the Beat: Story Structure for Romance Novels.* Gwen Hayes Media, 2016.

Hughes, Thomas. *Tom Brown's School Days.* London, 1857.

Jones, Diana Wynne. *The Tough Guide to Fantasyland.* Vista Books, 1996.

King, Stephen. *On Writing: A Memoir of the Craft.* Scribner, 2000.

The Mask. Directed by Charles Russell, performance by Jim Carrey, New Line Cinema, 1994.

Pierce, Tamora. *Protector of the Small.* Random House, 2004.

---. *Song of the Lioness* quartet. Atheneum Books, 1988.

Rowling, J.K. *Harry Potter.* Bloomsbury, 2007.
Tarantino, Quentin.
Vogler, Stephen. *The Writer's Journey: Mythic Structure for Storytellers and Screenwriters.* Michael Wiese Productions, 1992.

Chapter 4
Beer, Edith Hornik. "Memoir." Dorland Mountain Arts Colony, 22 Feb. 2020, Temecula, CA. Workshop.
Coyne, Shawn. *The Story Grid: What Good Editors Know.* Black Irish Entertainment, 2015.
Story Grid. 2020, storygrid.com.

Chapter 5
Brontë, Emily. *Wuthering Heights.* London, 1847.
Calvino, Italo. *If on a Winter's Night a Traveler.* Translated by William Weaver, Houghton Mifflin Harcourt, 1981.
Haddon, Mark. *The Curious Incident of the Dog in the Night-Time.* Jonathan Cape, 2003.
Lee, Harper. *Go Set a Watchman.* HarperCollins, 2015.
---. *To Kill a Mockingbird.* J. B. Lippincott & Co, 1960.
Meyer, Stephenie. *The Twilight Saga.* Little, Browne and Company, 2008.
---. *Eclipse.* Little, Browne and Company, 2007.
Rowling, J.K. *Harry Potter.* Bloomsbury, 2007.
Shakespeare, William. *The Winter's Tale.* London, 1623.

Chapter 6
Canning, Bridget. "Characterization." Fog Lit Festival, 30 Sept. 2017, Saint John Free Public Library. Workshop.
Haddon, Mark. *The Curious Incident of the Dog in the Night-Time.* Jonathan Cape, 2003.
Hodgins, Jack. *A Passion for Narrative: A Guide to Writing Fiction.* St. Martin's Press, 1994.

Laurence, Margaret.

Pagh, Nancy. *Write Moves: A Creative Writing Guide and Anthology*. Broadview Press, 2016.

Pirbhai, Mariam, and Waubgeshig Rice. "Ethically Writing Outside Yourself." Interview with Sanchari Sur. *Write,* vol. 48, no. 1, 2020.

Riordan, Rick. *The Heroes of Olympus.* Disney-Hyperion, 2014.

---. *The Lost Hero.* Disney-Hyperion, 2010.

Salinger, J. D. *The Catcher in the Rye.* Little, Brown and Company, 1951.

Shakespeare, William. *The Tragedy of Macbeth.* London, 1623.

Chapter 7

Brody, Jessica. *Save the Cat! Writes a Novel: The Last Book on Novel Writing You'll Ever Need.* Ten Speed Press, 2018.

Kinsella, Sophie. *Confessions of a Shopaholic.* Black Swan, 2000.

Shelley, Mary. *Frankenstein.* London, 1818.

Tolkien, J. R. R. *The Fellowship of the Ring.* George Allen & Unwin, 1954.

Chapter 8

Blanchot, Maurice. *The Writing of the Disaster.* Translated by Ann Smock, University of Nebraska Press, 1995.

Bohannon, Zach, and J. Thorn. "The Three Story Method Influencer Series." *The Career Author Podcast,* episodes 111-115, February-March 2020, thecareerauthor.com/podcast/.

Campbell, Joseph. *The Hero with a Thousand Faces.* Pantheon Books, 1949.

Cinderella. Directed by Clyde Geronimi, Hamilton Luske, and Wilfred Jackson, performances by Ilene Woods and William Phipps, Walt Disney Pictures and RKO Radio Pictures, 1950.

Daigle, Roland. *Alerte à Richibuctou.* Bouton d'or Acadie, 2019.

Forster, E. M. *Aspects of the Novel.* Edward Arnold, 1927.

Frozen. Directed by Jennifer Lee and Chris Buck, performances by Kristin Bell, Idina Menzel, Johnathan Groff, Santino Fontana, and Josh Gad, Walt Disney Pictures, 2013.

Guardians of the Galaxy. Directed by James Gunn, performances by Chris Pratt, Zoe Saldana, Dave Bautista, Vin Diesel, and Bradley Cooper, Marvel Studios and Walt Disney Studios, 2014.

Hayes, Gwen. *Romancing the Beat: Story Structure for Romance Novels.* Gwen Hayes Media, 2016.

Homer. *The Odyssey.*

Hudson, Kim. *The Virgin's Promise: Writing Stories of Feminine Creative, Spiritual and Sexual Awakening.* Michael Wiese Productions, 2010.

Milton, John. *Paradise Lost.* London, 1667.

Murdock, Maureen. *The Heroine's Journey: Woman's Quest for Wholeness*. Shambala, 1990.

Tolkien, J. R. R. *The Lord of the Rings.* George Allen & Unwin, 1955.

Vogler, Stephen. *The Writer's Journey: Mythic Structure for Storytellers and Screenwriters.* Michael Wiese Productions, 1992.

While You Were Sleeping. Directed by Jon Turteltaub, performances by Sandra Bullock and Bill Pullman, Hollywood Pictures and Buena Vista Pictures, 1995.

Wonder Woman. Directed by Patty Jenkins, performance by Gal Godot, DC Films and Warner Bros. Pictures, 2017.

Chapter 9

Campbell, Joseph. *The Hero with a Thousand Faces.* Pantheon Books, 1949.

Freud, Sigmund.

Hayes, Gwen. *Romancing the Beat: Story Structure for Romance Novels.* Gwen Hayes Media, 2016.

Jung, Carl.

Pagh, Nancy. *Write Moves: A Creative Writing Guide and Anthology.* Broadview Press, 2016.

Pirbhai, Mariam, and Waubgeshig Rice. "Ethically Writing Outside Yourself." Interview with Sanchari Sur. *Write,* vol. 48, no. 1, 2020.

Simone, Francina. "How to Write Diverse Characters | NaNoWriMo." *YouTube,* 5 Feb 2019, youtu.be/9qYsBwfrojQ.

Whedon, Joss, creator. *Buffy the Vampire Slayer.* Mutant Enemy Productions, 2003.

Vogler, Stephen. *The Writer's Journey: Mythic Structure for Storytellers and Screenwriters.* Michael Wiese Productions, 1992.

Chapter 10

Montgomery, Lucy Maude. *The Blue Castle.* McClelland and Stewart, 1926.

Vonnegut, Kurt. *Bagombo Snuff Box.* G. P. Putnam's Sons, 1999.

Chapter 11

Austen, Jane. *Pride and Prejudice.* London, 1813.

Clarke, George Elliott. Workshop in Fredericton, 2006.

Hodgins, Jack. *A Passion for Narrative: A Guide to Writing Fiction.* St. Martin's Press, 1994.

McKee, Robert. *Story: Substance, Structure, Style, and the Principles of Screenwriting.* ItBooks, 1997.

Pagh, Nancy. *Write Moves: A Creative Writing Guide and Anthology.* Broadview Press, 2016.

Schwenger, Peter. *Fantasm & Fiction: On Textual Envisioning.* Stanford UP, 1999.

Chapter 12

Clarke, George Elliott. “Poetry Workshop” Sept 21, 2007. Fredericton, NB.

McKee, Robert. *Story: Substance, Structure, Style, and the Principles of Screenwriting.* ItBooks, 1997.

Pagh, Nancy. *Write Moves: A Creative Writing Guide and Anthology.* Broadview Press, 2016.

Appendix 2

Many sources from Chapter 8, plus:

Beowulf. Trans. Seamus Heaney. Farrar, Straus and Giroux, 1999.

Booker, Christopher. *The Seven Basic Plots: Why We Tell Stories.* Continuum, 2004.

Dickens, Charles. *A Christmas Carol.* London, 1843.

Gabaldon, Diana. *Outlander.* Delacorte Press, 2014.

Gray, Harold. *Little Orphan Annie.* Tribune Media Services, 2010.

Homer. *The Iliad.*

Lewis, C. S. *The Voyage of the Dawn Treader.* Geoffrey Bles, 1952.

Meyer, Stephenie. *Twilight.* Little, Browne and Company, 2005.

Shaffer, Mary Ann. *The Guernsey Literary and Potato Peel Pie Society.* Dial Press, 2008.

Shakespeare, William. *The Tragedy of Macbeth.* London, 1623.

Whedon, Joss, creator. *Buffy the Vampire Slayer.* Mutant Enemy Productions, 2003.

About the Author

Kathy Mac loves dogs, helps run the Odd Sundays Reading Series in Fredericton New Brunswick, Canada, published her third poetry book *Human Misunderstanding* in 2017 and a book of essays (as Dr. Kathleen McConnell) in 2012, is starting to envy her retired friends though she still enjoys teaching creative writing at St. Thomas University, has won some regional and national writing awards and been nominated for more, has brown eyes, used to have brown hair, and has a website at kathymacpoet.com.

About the Project

Wording Around with Prose was published as part of the requirements for English 3153: Literary Publishing at St. Thomas University.

In the autumn of 2020, when classes could be taught only asynchronously online, the twelve students of Lit Pub went above and beyond in their pursuit of this project: Claude Chartier, Delaney Crawford, Neomi Iancu Haliva, Katy Johnson, Dominic Kent, Sara Lamk, Carly Mason, Erika Ruiz Arenas, Milly Squires, Caelin Sullivan, Rae Thomas, and Salima Tourkmani-MacDonald. Publishing warriors, all!

If you liked *Wording Around with Prose*, and want to hear about more Wording Around publications, drop an email to

wordingaroundpress@gmail.com

or go to our website at

wordingaround.com

CPSIA information can be obtained
at www.ICGtesting.com
Printed in the USA
LVHW081542230323
742311LV00025B/1273